BARBRA STREISAND

A Little Golden Book® Biography

By Judy Katschke
Illustrated by Brenna Vaughan

A GOLDEN BOOK • NEW YORK

Barbara Joan Streisand was born on April 24, 1942, in Brooklyn, New York, to a Jewish family. Her father was an English teacher. Her mother worked as a secretary and loved to sing. Her big brother, Sheldon, was seven years old when she was born.

No one knew that little Barbara would one day change the spelling of her name to Barbra *and* change the world as one of the most talented performers of all time!

But Barbra's life got off to a rough start. Soon after her first birthday, her father died. To make ends meet, Barbra's mother worked long hours, and she and the children moved in with her parents.

Not having a father made Barbra feel different from the other kids at school. She was shy and sometimes teased by her classmates.

But Barbra wasn't shy when it came to singing. She loved to sit on the stoop of her grandparents' building and belt out all kinds of songs. Singing made her happy. And hearing Barbra sing made others happy, too. The night she performed at a school PTA meeting, all the parents and teachers cheered!

When Barbra was eight years old, her mother remarried and soon had a baby girl named Rosalind. Barbra felt alone and ignored by her mother and stepfather. She spent hours watching movies, wondering what it would be like to be the characters on the screen.

At fourteen, Barbra saw her first Broadway show, *The Diary of Anne Frank*, which was about a Jewish girl in hiding with her family during World War II. After seeing the play, Barbra knew she wanted to be an actress!

When her school day ended, Barbra rode the subway from Brooklyn to Manhattan to take acting classes. She spent her summer vacations acting and singing in theater groups in upstate New York.

After high school graduation, her mother urged her to get a steady job as a secretary. But Barbra had other plans—she was going to be a famous performer!

Barbra and a friend moved into a small apartment in Manhattan. She was determined to make it on her own, without help from her family. Barbra went on auditions and earned money working as an office clerk, a theater usher, and a switchboard operator.

She entered a talent show at a nightclub called the Lion, hoping to win the fifty-dollar prize. To ease her nerves, Barbra used her acting skills and pretended to be a character while she sang.

The audience loved her. Barbra won the contest!
The Lion hired her to perform there two nights a week.
Soon, Barbra was singing at other clubs in the city.

In 1961, nineteen-year-old Barbra auditioned for the Broadway musical *I Can Get It for You Wholesale*. The director was so impressed, he gave her the role of Miss Marmelstein, even though it was originally written for a fifty-year-old!

Barbra's part was small, but her singing and comedic timing stole the show. She received a Tony Award nomination in 1962 for Best Performance by a Featured Actress in a Musical. That same year, Barbra signed her first record deal.

The year 1963 was a big one for Barbra. She performed for President John F. Kennedy at the White House Correspondents' Association Dinner. Millions of viewers tuned in to *The Judy Garland Show* to hear Barbra and Judy sing "Happy Days Are Here Again" and "Get Happy."

    And in September of that year, the twenty-one-year-old rising star married her first husband, actor Elliott Gould. The newlyweds had a lot in common. They were both from Jewish families and born in Brooklyn, and they had both starred in the same Broadway show. A few years later, they became parents to a baby boy they named Jason.

Barbra returned to Broadway in 1964, playing the role of comedian Fanny Brice in the musical *Funny Girl*. Audiences loved the show and the songs "Don't Rain on My Parade" and "People."

A few years later, *Funny Girl* became a Hollywood movie. Even though she had never been in a movie, Barbra was chosen to be the star. Once again, Barbra was a hit! The film won eight Academy Awards, including Best Actress for Barbra. Proudly holding her Oscar, she gazed down at the gold statue and said the words she made famous in the film: "Hello, gorgeous!"

Barbra went on to star in more movies. There were romantic dramas like *The Way We Were*, comedies such as *What's Up, Doc?*, and lavish musicals like *Hello, Dolly!* For the royal performance of *Funny Lady*, the sequel to *Funny Girl*, Barbra was greeted by England's Queen Elizabeth II!

By the 1980s, Barbra was at the top of her game, but she wanted to do more than act and sing. Barbra wanted to direct!

Barbra's directorial debut was a movie musical called *Yentl,* based on a short story about a Jewish girl in the early 1900s who pretends to be a boy so she could study religion in school. The story was very important to Barbra, and she worked hard to get the movie made just as she wanted.

Yentl was a 1983 box office success—and Barbra was the first woman in history to write, produce, direct, and star in a Hollywood film!

Barbra is the only singer to have a number one album six decades in a row! But for twenty-seven years, fans couldn't see her perform live. Barbra bravely admitted that she suffered from stage fright ever since she forgot the lines to a song at her concert in New York's Central Park.

Thankfully, she worked on her fears and went on tour in 1993, starting with a sold-out New Year's Eve show in Las Vegas.

When Barbra isn't performing, writing, or producing, she's very active in causes she believes in. Her Streisand Foundation supports dozens of charities for animals, equal rights, education, and the environment. In 2012, she founded the Barbra Streisand Women's Heart Center at Cedars-Sinai Hospital in Los Angeles.

To thank her for all the good she has done, in 2015, President Barack Obama awarded Barbra with the highest civilian honor in the United States—the Presidential Medal of Freedom.

Barbra lives in Malibu, California, with her second husband, actor James Brolin. The home they share is both beautiful and fun. There are many buildings on their property, including one with a mini shopping mall in the basement!

There's an old-fashioned sweet shop that serves popcorn and frozen yogurt, a dress shop displaying her costumes, and a shop for her antique doll collection. Barbra never had a doll as a child—now she has many!

In her garden, there's a wishing well, blooming with flowers. Barbra Streisand was once a little girl in Brooklyn who wished to be a famous performer. Fans all around the world are very glad her wish came true!